OCEAN FOOD CHAINS

Heidi Moore

Chicago, Illinois

www.heinemannraintree.com
Visit our website to find out more information about Heinemann-Raintree books.

To order:
☎ Phone 888-454-2279
🖳 Visit www.heinemannraintree.com to browse our catalog and order online.

©2011 Heinemann Library
an imprint of Capstone Global Library, LLC
Chicago, Illinois

Edited by Abby Colich and Andrew Farrow
Designed by Victoria Allen
Illustrated by Words and Publications
Picture research by Mica Brancic
Originated by Capstone Global Library, Ltd.
Printed by China Translation & Printing Services, Ltd.

14 13 12 11 10
10 9 8 7 6 5 4 3 2 1

Library of Congress Cataloging-in-Publication Data
Moore, Heidi, 1976-
  Ocean food chains / Heidi Moore.
    p. cm. -- (Protecting food chains)
  Includes bibliographical references and index.
  ISBN 978-1-4329-3859-8 (hc) -- ISBN 978-1-4329-3866-6 (pb) 1. Marine ecology--Juvenile literature. 2. Food chains (Ecology)--Juvenile literature. I. Title.
  QH541.5.S3M64 2011
  577.7'16--dc22
                        2009049547

Acknowledgments
Alamy pp. 15 (©Michael Patrick O'Neill), 19 (©blickwinkel/Hartl), 39 (©Visual&Written SL); Corbis pp. 34 (©Joe McDonald), 36 (©Paul Souders); FLPA p. 23 (Colin Marshall); Getty Images pp. 41 (AFP Photo/Adrian Dennis), 42 (altrendo nature); Photolibrary pp. 4 (age fotostock/Marevision Marevision), 8 (WaterFrame - Underwater Images/Reinhard Dirscherl), 9 (Oxford Scientific (OSF)/Paulo de Oliveira), 13 (Oxford Scientific (OSF)/R. Pingree), 14 (Pacific Stock/Perrine Doug), 17 (Phototake Science/Roland Birke), 18 (Oxford Scientific (OSF)/Richard Hermann), 21 (Oxford Scientific (OSF)/Paulo de Oliveira), 22 (Oxford Scientific (OSF)/Daniel J Cox), 25 (WaterFrame - Underwater Images/Reinhard Dirscherl), 26 (WaterFrame - Underwater Images/Mirko Zanni), 27 (imagebroker.net/Geophoto/Natalia Chervyakova), 28 (All Canada Photos/Wayne Lynch), 29 (WaterFrame - Underwater Images/Reinhard Dirscherl), 31 (WaterFrame - Underwater Images/Wolfgang Poelzer), 33 (age fotostock/Gonzalo Azumendi), 35 (fStop/Frederick Bass), 37 (Animals Animals/Shane Moore), 43 (MIXA Co., Ltd.); Photoshot p. 40.

Cover photograph of a Corkwing Wrasse (Symphodus melops) reproduced with permission of Photolibrary (age fotostock/Marevision Marevision).

Cover and spread background image reproduced with permission of Shutterstock (©Strejman).

We would like to thank Kenneth Dunton and Dana Sjostrom for their invaluable help in the preparation of this book.

CONTENTS

Some words are shown in bold, **like this**. You can find out what they mean by looking in the glossary.

WHAT IS AN OCEAN FOOD CHAIN?

The Hawaiian Islands sit in the warm waters of the Pacific Ocean. Look below the surface of the water. There is an underwater world.

Tiny plants called **phytoplankton** take in **energy** from the Sun. Tiny animals called **zooplankton** feed on the phytoplankton. Crabs scuttle along the ocean floor, gobbling up zooplankton. A yellowfin goatfish digs through the sand. It catches a small crab and swallows it whole. Suddenly a **reef** shark swims out from inside a cave. Gulp! It eats the goatfish in one bite.

In time this shark will die. Then **decomposers** such as **bacteria** will break down the shark's body. Decomposers break down dead plant and animal material. This releases the energy from the plants and animals back into the water and soil. Soon other living things will take in that energy, and the cycle will begin again.

A ballan wrasse fish devours a crab in an ocean food chain.

FOOD CHAIN

This cycle is called a food chain. A food chain shows how energy moves from one **organism** to another. An organism is any living thing. Energy moves between living things when one organism feeds on another.

Sometimes this process is shown using a food chain diagram. A food chain diagram has a series of arrows. The arrows show how each member of the chain gets its energy. Energy moves from the food to the animal that eats it. For example, in the Hawaiian food chain to the right, the arrow leads from the phytoplankton to the zooplankton, from the zooplankton to the humpback whale, and so on.

Each link in a food chain is important. When something happens to one link, it affects the entire chain. Humans depend on oceans, too, even though we have been harming them. It is important to protect ocean food chains.

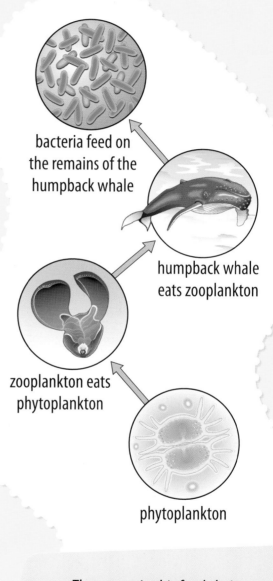

bacteria feed on the remains of the humpback whale

humpback whale eats zooplankton

zooplankton eats phytoplankton

phytoplankton

The arrows in this food chain diagram show how energy is transferred from one organism to another.

WHAT ARE THE PARTS OF A FOOD CHAIN?

Food chains are usually made up of four parts: **producers**, **primary consumers**, **secondary consumers**, and decomposers. All food chains begin with plants, which are producers. Plants make their own food in a process called **photosynthesis**. This means they use energy from the Sun to make their food. Then plants become food for other organisms.

Primary consumers eat plants. **Consumers** that eat only plants are called **herbivores**. Secondary consumers eat primary consumers. Secondary consumers can be **carnivores**, which eat only animals. Or they can be **omnivores**, which eat both plants and animals.

Decomposers and **scavengers** break down dead plants and animals into **nutrients**. These nutrients go back into the environment for other producers to absorb.

You may have heard the terms "**predator**" and "**prey**." A predator is an animal that eats another animal. The prey is the animal that is eaten.

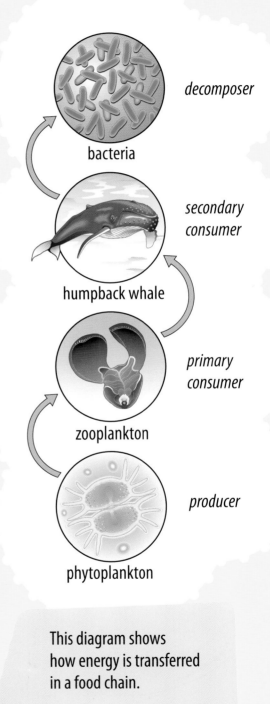

decomposer

bacteria

secondary consumer

humpback whale

primary consumer

zooplankton

producer

phytoplankton

This diagram shows how energy is transferred in a food chain.

WHAT IS A FOOD WEB?

Food chains only tell one part of the story. They show just one series of links. Many organisms eat—or are eaten by—more than one type of organism, creating more than one food chain. A food web diagram shows how food chains are linked together. It looks a bit like a spider web. The arrows show how energy moves from organism to organism. It tells you who eats whom. In the food web below, herring is food for both tuna and sharks. An animal can be in more than one food chain. An animal can also be both a primary and secondary consumer.

This food web shows how ocean organisms are connected.

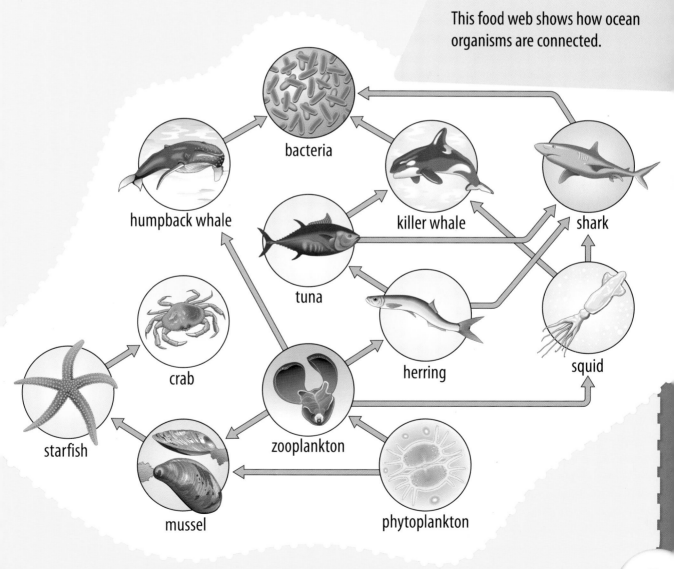

bacteria

humpback whale

killer whale

shark

tuna

crab

herring

squid

starfish

zooplankton

mussel

phytoplankton

WHAT IS AN OCEAN HABITAT?

Oceans, seas, and gulfs cover almost three-fourths of Earth. There are five major oceans—the Pacific, Atlantic, Indian, Southern (Antarctic), and Arctic oceans. (You can see them on the map on pages 10–11.)

The oceans are rich with life. Thousands of **species** (types) of plants and animals live in the oceans. We already know of more than 20,000 species of fish. Many forms of life are still unknown to us, especially in the deepest parts of the ocean. Scientists discover new species all the time.

Within each ocean, there are many different **habitats**. A habitat is a place where **organisms** live. Organisms depend on their habitat for food, shelter, and everything else they need to survive.

All living things are **adapted** to their habitat. If a fish lives in warm water, then it is adapted to warm water. It likely could not survive in cold water. If a plant lives near the surface and needs lots of sunlight, then it is adapted to shallow water. It likely would not survive in the deep sea. Over time organisms develop **adaptations** that help them survive in certain habitats.

Warm ocean water surrounds the islands of Micronesia.

This great squid lives in the deep water of the Mediterranean Sea.

DEEP SEA

Few organisms live in the deep sea. It is difficult to survive there. At about 900 meters (3,000 feet) below sea level, there is no sunlight at all. Many fish that live in the deep sea do not have eyes. Others, like the giant squid, have huge eyes. These are adaptations to living so far underwater.

WHERE IN THE WORLD ARE OCEAN HABITATS?

This map shows the location of the main oceans of the world.

NORTH
AMERICA

ATLANTIC
OCEAN

PACIFIC
OCEAN

SOUTH
AMERICA

ARCTIC OCEAN

NORTH
SEA

EUROPE

ASIA

AFRICA

PACIFIC
OCEAN

INDIAN
OCEAN

AUSTRALIA

ANTARCTIC OCEAN

ANTARCTICA

WHAT ARE THE PRODUCERS IN OCEANS?

Producers, or plants, turn **energy** from the Sun into food. They do this by **photosynthesis**. Photosynthesis is a process plants use to produce food from sunlight.

Producers are at the very beginning of the food chain. All **consumers** depend on producers in some way. Some consumers eat producers. Some eat other consumers that eat producers. If the producers disappeared, the consumers would, too. It would affect the entire food chain.

PHYTOPLANKTON

The main producers in the ocean are **phytoplankton**. Phytoplankton are tiny, plantlike **organisms**. There are thousands of different **species** of phytoplankton. The most abundant group of phytoplankton are called **diatoms**.

All types of phytoplankton need sunlight, water, carbon dioxide, and **nutrients** to grow. Phytoplankton, like all plants, contain a substance called **chlorophyll**. Chlorophyll is what makes plants green. It helps plants trap sunlight to use in photosynthesis.

Phytoplankton live near the surface of the water. Moving **currents** of water bring nutrients from the sea floor up to the phytoplankton. Then small fish and some types of whale feed on the phytoplankton.

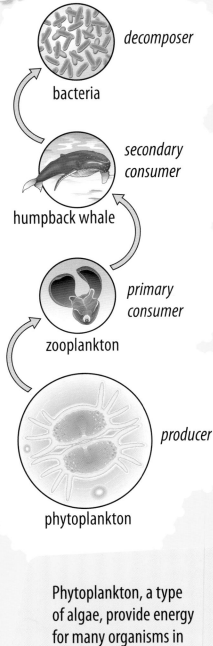

decomposer

bacteria

secondary consumer

humpback whale

primary consumer

zooplankton

producer

phytoplankton

Phytoplankton, a type of algae, provide energy for many organisms in an ocean.

RED TIDE

One type of phytoplankton, the dinoflagellates, contains toxins (poison). Sometimes a lot of dinoflagellates grow quickly in one area of the ocean. The large cloud of dinoflagellates turns the water reddish-brown. This is called a red tide. Red tides often happen in areas of warm water or very low salt. In large enough numbers, a red tide can kill fish. It can even make people who eat shellfish sick, because shellfish absorb more of the toxins.

WHAT'S IN A NAME?

The word "**plankton**" is from a Greek word meaning "wanderer." Phytoplankton got their name because they wander, or move around, in the ocean.

A red tide floats near the coast of Plymouth, England.

FROM PHYTOPLANKTON TO SEAWEEDS

Phytoplankton are a form of algae. Have you ever seen algae? If you have a fish tank and ever forgot to clean it, algae might have grown on the walls. Algae grows just about anywhere. It grows on rocky coastlines and on the floor of shallow pools. It also grows in soil and in rivers and lakes. In the ocean, algae floats along, taking in nutrients.

There are four main types of algae:
- green
- brown
- red
- golden or golden-brown (which are called diatoms).

One larger type of algae is seaweed. It usually grows in shallow water at depths of 50 meters (165 feet) or less. Here it is closer to the sunlight that it needs to grow. Seaweed grows attached to the ocean floor by **holdfast growths**. Giant kelp, a type of seaweed, can grow 30 meters (100 feet) long. Kelp's flexibility and tough, leathery **fronds** are **adaptations** that help it survive in rough ocean waters.

This giant sea kelp forest grows off the coast of California.

Sargasso Seaweed

A huge area of floating seaweed lies between the United States and Africa in the Atlantic Ocean. This area is called the Sargasso Sea. It is made up of brown algae. The Sargasso Sea is almost as large as a continent—and it travels! The wind and currents move it around in the ocean.

This photo shows an area of Sargasso seaweed.

A Broken Chain: El Niño

A change in the weather can affect ocean food chains. During the El Niño weather pattern, the surface waters of the Pacific Ocean grow warmer. This warmer water does not move around as much. Cold currents from the ocean floor cannot reach the surface. Then phytoplankton do not get the nutrients they need to survive. As the phytoplankton die, the fish and whales that feed on them cannot find enough food. Without enough food, some of these animals die.

WHAT ARE THE PRIMARY CONSUMERS IN OCEANS?

A food chain has many levels. **Producers** make up the first level. Any **organism** above the level of producer is a **consumer**. Consumers feed on producers or other consumers.

Above the producers in the food chain are the **primary consumers**. They make up the second level. Primary consumers feed on producers. They are **herbivores**.

The most common primary consumer in the ocean is **zooplankton**. Zooplankton are tiny animals that float in the ocean. There are many different types of zooplankton. Some are tiny, shrimplike creatures, and others are the **larvae** (young) of jellyfish and other fish that grow up to be larger animals.

Nearly all fish feed on zooplankton when they are young. Some depend on zooplankton for food their entire lives. Zooplankton feed on **phytoplankton**, **bacteria**, or other zooplankton.

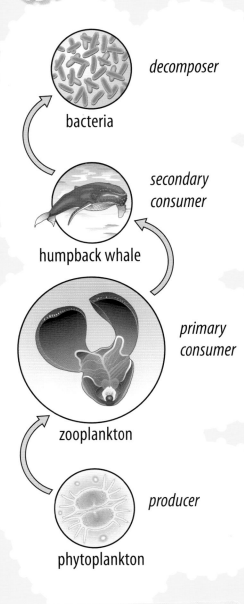

decomposer

bacteria

secondary consumer

humpback whale

primary consumer

zooplankton

producer

phytoplankton

HOW MANY?
One drop of ocean water can hold thousands of zooplankton.

Consumers such as zooplankton feed on plants.

Copepods are tiny, shrimplike zooplankton.

COPEPODS

Copepods are one type of zooplankton. They are small **crustaceans**, or shrimplike organisms. There are about 12,000 **species** (types) of copepod.

There are probably more copepods in the world than any other organism. In fact, there may be more copepods in the world than all other animals combined. Scientists cannot count them all because they are very tiny. Some are as small as a speck of dust. Others are as large as a grain of rice.

They push themselves through the water with their long antennae and paddle-like limbs. They feed on **diatoms** and other types of phytoplankton. Larvae, bigger fish, and some whales eat copepods.

KRILL

Another type of zooplankton is **krill**. These are small, pinkish-red crustaceans. Krill are larger than copepods. They are about the size of your thumb. Krill have up to 13 pairs of legs. They use their back pairs of legs for movement and the front pairs for feeding. Krill eat mostly phytoplankton. Special filter baskets below their eyes capture phytoplankton.

Krill have a very important role in the ocean food chain. Many types of fish, seabirds, and baleen whales depend on krill for food. In Russia, Japan, and other countries, anglers catch tons and tons of krill each year. They use the krill for bait and for fish food. In some countries, people munch on krill as a special dish!

ANTARCTIC KRILL

Between 125 million and 6 billion tons of krill live in the Antarctic Ocean. Certain times of year, very large swarms of krill can be seen from space!

Krill are a very important part of the Antarctic Ocean food chain. Without them, most other species in the Antarctic would die out.

Thousands of krill cluster in a small area of the ocean.

WEIGHTY MATTER

Scientists think the total weight of Antarctic krill is more than the total weight of all humans on Earth.

LOSING A LINK: ANTARCTIC KRILL

Antarctic krill levels have dropped by about 80 percent since the 1970s. Many Antarctic krill depend on algae that live on the sea ice. **Global warming** has caused much of this sea ice to melt. This means there are fewer algae for krill to feed on. If krill numbers keep falling, the entire Antarctic food chain will be at risk.

Krill are an important link in Antarctic Ocean food chains.

WHAT ARE THE SECONDARY CONSUMERS IN OCEANS?

Secondary consumers feed on **primary consumers**. They are ocean **predators**. They range from a small herring to a giant shark.

OCTOPUS

An octopus has a soft, rounded body and eight arms. Suction cups on the arms help it trap **prey**. The octopus eats mostly crabs, shrimp, and mussels. In a fight, it can squirt out a cloud of ink, then swim away. Some octopuses can **camouflage** (mask) themselves. They can change color or make spots appear. This helps them catch prey or hide from predators.

JELLYFISH

Jellyfish have no skeleton. Most of their body is a jellylike mass. Many are clear, but they also can be blue, brown, pink, or white. Stinging tentacles help them capture prey. They mostly feed on small fish and **zooplankton**.

FLATFISH

Flatfish include many fish people like to eat, such as flounder, halibut, and sole. True to their name, flatfish are flat. They swim with one side facing up and one side facing down. Their eyes are on one side of their body. Flatfish prey includes clams, shrimp, squid, and marine worms.

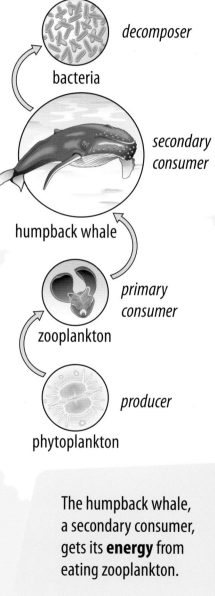

decomposer

bacteria

secondary consumer

humpback whale

primary consumer

zooplankton

producer

phytoplankton

The humpback whale, a secondary consumer, gets its **energy** from eating zooplankton.

This barbeled dragonfish lurks in the deep sea, waiting to sink its sharp teeth into prey.

DEEP-SEA PREDATORS

Some bizarre predators call the deep sea home. Creatures there develop unusual features to help them find or capture prey. Some glow with **bioluminescence**. Because sunlight does not reach the deep sea, these creatures make their own light. This light can confuse potential predators.

The fierce viperfish uses tiny lights to lure fish and **crustaceans** close. The viperfish's long, sharp teeth trap the prey in its mouth. The eel-like dragonfish finds prey using glowing spots beneath its eyes. The anglerfish uses a glowing pole on the tip of its nose to attract fish. Then it closes its powerful jaws on its catch.

These killer whales are hunting porpoises in southeastern Alaska.

TOP OCEAN PREDATORS

Do any creatures feed on secondary consumers? Yes. These are the top predators in the ocean food chain. Some call them **tertiary consumers**, meaning "third-level **consumers**."

The killer whale, or orca, is one of the most successful ocean predators. It eats fish, squid, sea lions, seals, and seabirds. A killer whale is not very large compared to most whales. It is only about 9 meters (30 feet) long. But it will attack other whales two or three times its size.

Many people—and, likely, ocean creatures—fear the great white shark. It is a large and dangerous predator. Great whites range in size from 6 to 8 meters (19 to 26 feet). They can weigh up to 2,100 kilograms (4,600 pounds). Fast and strong, great white sharks cut through the water to attack their prey. With sharp, triangle-shaped teeth, they tear into prey such as squid, halibut, tuna, porpoises, and sea lions.

Another top predator is . . . you! We are one of the top predators of ocean **species**. Humans eat millions of tons of fish each year.

LOSING A LINK: THE SAND EEL

A key ocean predator, the sand eel, is disappearing. The sand eel is a small, eel-like fish. It an important part of the food chain in the waters of the North Sea. Sand eels are dying out because of **overfishing** and rising ocean temperatures. Seabirds, whales, and other animals depend on sand eels for food. Some species of seabird are finding it tough to get enough to eat. Its decline is affecting the fishing industry as well. Now people are taking steps to protect the sand eel and save this important link.

The number of sand eels is dropping. This will affect food chains in the North Sea.

WHAT ARE THE DECOMPOSERS IN OCEANS?

Decomposers are an important link in the ocean food chain. They play a key role in the process of life and death. Decomposers break down dead plant and animal matter. This frees up **nutrients** for the food chain. Then ocean **producers** consume these nutrients, and the food chain process can continue.

This process is a bit like recycling. When we put out glass bottles to be recycled, the glass can be used again to make other things. When decomposers break down matter, it can be used again.

Without decomposers, the waste would pile up. Soon the entire ocean would be filled with dead matter.

BACTERIA

Bacteria are the main ocean decomposers. These are very simple but important **organisms**. Bacteria are single-celled organisms. (Cells are the smallest units of living things.) Some bacteria are shaped like rods, and others are spirals.

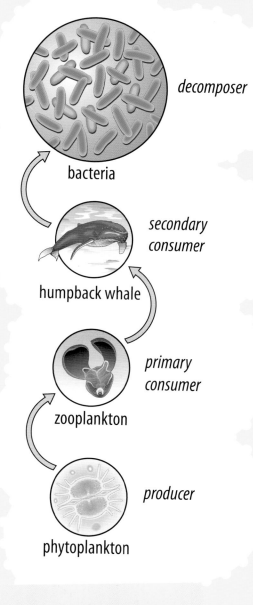

decomposer

bacteria

secondary consumer

humpback whale

primary consumer

zooplankton

producer

phytoplankton

Decomposers are a small but important link in ocean food chains.

A lobster, one type of scavenger, scoops up material from the ocean floor.

Most bacteria are so tiny you could not see them without a microscope. In fact, a million bacteria fit on the head of a pin. Bacteria help break down dead matter into substances other organisms can use. Some bacteria live in the digestive systems of ocean organisms and help them break down food. Other bacteria live on **feces** (poo) and help break it down.

SCAVENGER HUNT

Scavengers feed on dead animals. They swim or walk or slither around looking for decaying (rotting) matter. Many scavengers, such as crabs and lobsters, are bottom feeders. They live on the ocean floor. Some scavengers have claws that help them scoop material off the ocean floor. Some sharks are scavengers. They eat wounded or dead creatures.

A Spanish shawl nudibranch floats in the Pacific Ocean.

STRANGE SCAVENGERS

Some of the strangest-looking creatures in the ocean are scavengers.

Sea cucumbers look a bit like a cucumber. But they have soft bodies and may be pale and dark or brightly colored. They scoot along the ocean floor, feeding on waste. Some sea cucumbers have an unusual means of defense. They can shoot out internal organs through their **anus**. The sticky organs trap their attacker.

Sea anemones come in many bright colors and sizes. They grow attached to rocks or coral **reefs** on the ocean floor. Most **prey** on fish that swim too close. The sea anemone reaches out with its stinging tentacles. Then it moves the stunned prey into its mouth. Some sea anemones are scavengers. They eat green algae and other dead plant and animal matter.

Sea slugs look like a snail without a shell. One especially odd type of sea slug is the nudibranch. Its crazy patterns, shapes, and colors help it stand out from other **species**. Most sea slugs are **carnivores** that eat anemones, sponges, and corals. But some eat algae that they scrape off the sea floor.

A Broken Chain: Red King Crabs

One scavenger is causing problems in part of the Arctic Ocean. In the 1960s, Russia dumped red king crabs into the Barents Sea so that people would have a new creature to fish for. The king crab did not live there before. The crabs have no natural enemies in the Arctic, so their numbers grew quickly. Now the invaders have spread to Norway. The giant crabs eat many important creatures, including sea urchins, starfish, and mollusks. Today, the entire Barents Sea food chain is at risk.

A red king crab clings to a rock in the Barents Sea.

WHAT ARE OCEAN FOOD CHAINS LIKE AROUND THE WORLD?

Ocean **habitats** share many features, but they are not all the same. Different **species** live in warm, shallow seas than in cold, deep waters. Temperatures, **currents**, and the depth of the water all affect what species live in that area. Food chains differ in each part of the world.

THE ARCTIC OCEAN

The cold Arctic Ocean is the smallest ocean in the world. The frigid North Pole sits at its center. Near the North Pole is a floating sheet of ice several hundred miles wide.

Arctic dwellers are hardy animals. They are **adapted** to survive the harsh cold. Deepwater Arctic cod eat everything from **zooplankton** and fish eggs to **crustaceans** and worms.

Polar bears live here, too. They are huge animals. Males can weigh 600 kilograms (1,300 pounds). Females can weigh 300 kilograms (650 pounds). They are fierce **carnivores**. Polar bears hunt mostly seals and sometimes walruses or fish. They swim long distances, looking for food. Polar bears appear white, but their fur is actually transparent. The transparent fur traps heat and keeps them warm. Black skin underneath also absorbs sunlight to help them stay warm.

This polar bear has caught a seal.

A hawksbill turtle feeds on jellyfish in the Indian Ocean.

THE INDIAN OCEAN

The Indian Ocean lies between Africa, Asia, and Australia. It is the world's third largest ocean. It is more than five times the size of the United States.

The most common fish in the Indian Ocean include lantern fish, anchovies, sailfish, and several species of flying fish. Olive ridley sea turtles nest in the waters surrounding India and Sri Lanka, eating rock lobsters, jellyfish, and shrimp. Birds such as albatross and frigate birds feed on Indian Ocean fish.

THE ANTARCTIC OCEAN

The Antarctic Ocean is the fourth largest ocean in the world. It surrounds the continent of Antarctica. Many seabirds live there. Emperor and Adélie penguins search for food up and down the coastline. Gentoo and chinstrap penguins live along the coast and on some islands. Penguins are great swimmers and catch their food underwater. They mostly eat **krill** and small fish.

Several species of seal breed in the Antarctic. There are fur seals, huge elephant seals, and the common crabeater seal. Crabeater seals spend their time on the ice sheet. Leopard seals hunt and eat penguins. The Weddell seal can dive 600 meters (2,000 feet) below the surface and spend up to an hour underwater.

Common Antarctic Ocean fish species include Antarctic cod and icefish. Antarctic fish species can stand water temperatures as low as –2°C (28°F). At that temperature, a person would freeze to death in less than 15 minutes.

The most important link in the Antarctic food chain is krill. Squid, seabirds, seals, and whales all depend on krill for survival.

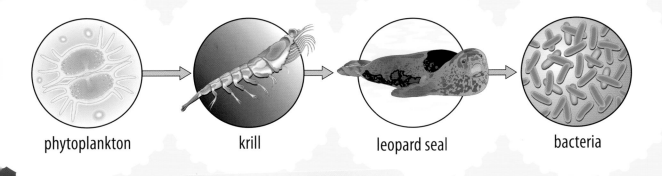

phytoplankton   krill   leopard seal   bacteria

This is an example of a food chain in the Antarctic Ocean.

The manta ray is less dangerous than it looks. It eats only plankton.

THE SOUTH PACIFIC

Between South America and Australia lies the South Pacific Ocean. Fiji, Tahiti, and other islands sit within this blue expanse. The water of the South Pacific is very clear.

Skates and rays, close relatives of the shark, swim the waters of this ocean. They eat mostly bony fish and shelled animals from the ocean floor. The huge manta ray looks dangerous but feeds only on **plankton**. The stonefish uses **camouflage** to blend into its rocky habitat. It waits for a small fish to swim by. Then, ouch! It stabs the **prey** with its poisonous back spines.

THE GREAT BARRIER REEF

The Great Barrier **Reef** lies off the northeast coast of Australia. It is the largest coral reef in the world. The name makes it sound like it is just one reef. Actually, it is a system of about 2,900 reefs. It stretches about 2,000 kilometers (1,250 miles). That is about the same length as the entire west coast of the United States.

Reefs are systems of coral. Corals are tiny **organisms** with bone-like shells. When a coral dies, its shell remains. Other corals attach to it. Over tens of thousands or millions of years, the coral builds up to form huge reefs.

Coral reefs are abundant with **producers** that need sunlight that can reach shallow waters. About 500 different species of seaweed grow near the Great Barrier Reef. This helps attract many types of fish, some of which feed on the seaweed. About 1,500 species of fish live in or near the Great Barrier Reef. Many are brightly colored or patterned.

One such fish is the clownfish. These small fish eat zooplankton and algae. Clownfish live among anemone. The anemone's poisonous tentacles do not harm the clownfish. In exchange for cleaning the anemone, the clownfish gets protection from **predators**.

Sea turtles, sea snakes, and giant clams live around the Great Barrier Reef, too. Lumpy, gray dugongs—a relative of the manatee—munch on underwater grasses.

This is a food chain from the Great Barrier Reef.

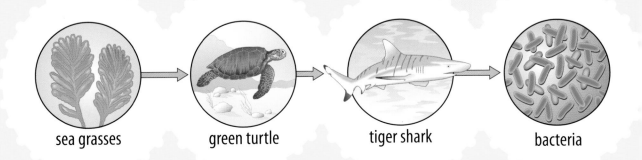

sea grasses　　　green turtle　　　tiger shark　　　bacteria

A Broken Chain: Reef at Risk

Today, the Great Barrier Reef is threatened. Rising ocean temperatures are killing off the delicate coral organisms. One Australian study says that 95 percent of the coral will die by 2050 if temperatures continue to rise. This would put many species that live near the reef at risk.

The Great Barrier Reef of Australia spreads out over 2,000 kilometers (1,250 miles).

HOW ARE HUMANS HARMING OCEAN FOOD CHAINS?

All over the world, ocean food chains are in trouble. Changes in temperature, water level, and acid levels are affecting the ocean's **organisms**. Human activity has put the world's oceans at risk.

POLLUTED WATERS

Harmful waste known as **pollution** affects the air, land, and water. Sometimes the ocean is **polluted** directly, such as when a cruise ship dumps waste into the sea. Pollution from factories, farms, and cities far away also harms the ocean. Chemicals and other waste pollute nearby rivers and streams, which flow into the ocean.

Plastic waste poses a big problem in the water. Plastic litter from diapers, shopping bags, and other sources floats on the ocean's surface. Sea turtles and seabirds get trapped in the plastic or swallow it and die. Scientists say each square mile of the ocean contains about 46,000 pieces of plastic litter.

This bird has been trapped by plastic litter.

Pollution also causes rising acid levels. Oceans absorb tons of carbon dioxide each year. As the gas dissolves, it makes the water more acidic. Higher acid levels harm shellfish and eat away at coral reefs. Some scientists think 40 years from now the oceans will be too acidic to support coral reefs.

LOSING A LINK: POISON IN FISH

Pollution has led to high mercury levels in some types of fish. Mercury is a metal found in nature. But in high levels, it is **toxic** (poisonous) to humans. Mercury from factories has found its way into the oceans. Some **species** of large fish now contain high levels. People who eat too much of these fish can get sick. However, fish contains healthy fats and oils. Fish that are low in mercury can be a part of a healthy diet.

Some types of seafood, such as crabs, contain less mercury than other types.

Warmer temperatures have caused polar ice to melt. Polar bears drown without enough polar ice to stop and rest on while swimming through the ocean looking for food.

CLIMATE CHANGE

Pollution contributes to changes in Earth's **climate**. **Climate change** is causing sea levels to rise. This puts coastal areas at risk and affects the flow of **currents**. It also has led to melting polar ice. Today, polar bears have to swim miles and miles between ice sheets to find food. They are at risk of dying out. Fish that depend on ice algae also are at risk.

A BROKEN CHAIN: ALIEN INVASION

Not all **aliens** are from outer space. Alien species, which are species brought into a new habitat, cause problems in the oceans. In the new habitat, they compete with **native** species for food. With no natural predators, their numbers often grow quickly. This is what happened with the red king crab in the Barents Sea (see page 27).

FISHED OUT

Another major threat to ocean **habitats** is **overfishing**. Modern equipment can capture more fish than nature can replace. This can cause levels of certain **species** to fall dangerously low.

When one species becomes scarce or dies out, the species that feed on it are at risk. Top **predators** such as tuna, swordfish, and halibut are especially at risk from overfishing. Since the 1950s, about 90 percent of these predators have been fished out.

Overfishing is a difficult issue. Many people depend on fishing for money and food. But overfishing can harm the fisheries, too. In the waters off Newfoundland, Canada, the cod population collapsed in 1992. Cod fisheries went out of business. About 40,000 people lost their jobs.

Too much fishing can harm ocean food chains.

DISASTER IN THE OCEAN!

Pollution, climate change, and overfishing happen over time. But some disasters hit a food chain all of a sudden.

Oil spills take a terrible toll on ocean food chains. They are hard to clean up, and their effects can last for years. What causes an oil spill? Human mistakes, wars, and storms all can cause oil spills.

RECENT OIL SPILLS

2005
Hurricane Katrina caused oil spills near New Orleans, Louisiana. Damaged pipelines, storage tanks, and oil plants leaked about 26 million liters (7 million gallons) of oil into the Gulf of Mexico.

2006
An oil tanker carrying 2 million liters (530,000 gallons) of oil sank off the coast of Guimaras Island in the Philippines. The tanker sank in deep water, which made it difficult to reach.

2007
A barge came loose from its tug boat and smashed into the *Hebei Spirit* oil tanker near South Korea. About 10 million liters (2.8 million gallons) of **crude oil** spilled near the coast.

2010
An explosion on a BP offshore drilling rig in the Gulf of Mexico killed 11 workers and caused millions of gallons of oil to leak into the Gulf, killing marine life such as sea birds and turtles and affecting the area's seafood industry.

Crews work to clean up oil left on the Alaskan coastline after the Exxon *Valdez* disaster.

EXXON *VALDEZ* DISASTER

On March 24, 1989, a terrible disaster took place in the Pacific Ocean near Alaska. The Exxon *Valdez* oil tanker ran into land in Prince William Sound. It spilled about 41 million liters (10.9 million gallons) of oil.

It was the largest oil spill ever in U.S. waters. About 1,770 kilometers (1,100 miles) of Alaskan coastline were damaged. The spill killed about 250,000 seabirds, up to 2,800 sea otters, and 302 harbor seals. Despite a major clean-up, some species never came back to their previous numbers.

WHAT CAN YOU DO TO PROTECT OCEAN FOOD CHAINS?

The oceans are some of the most beautiful—and important—places on Earth. Oceans are home to many different **species** of plants and animals. Preserving ocean **habitats** is the only way to ensure that the amazing **organisms** of the ocean survive.

Today, the oceans are at risk. What can you do to help protect them?

HELP CUT DOWN ON POLLUTION

Reducing **pollution** is the best way to keep the oceans healthy. Write letters to the people who represent you in government. Tell them to reduce pollution and keep the waterways clean. Ask your parents to do the same.

Scientists believe that 80 percent of the pollution in the ocean comes from land. Never dump anything into streams or rivers—or throw litter into the ocean. Support **organic** farms that do not use chemicals on their land. (The chemicals eventually make their way into the ocean.)

There is a lot you can do in your own home to cut down on waste. Recycle paper, plastic, glass, and aluminum. Do not waste water. Turn off the water while brushing your teeth.

If you live near or visit an ocean, you can help protect ocean food chains by picking up litter and not littering in the first place!

ROBOT FISH

Scientists in the United Kingdom are working on a new way to monitor ocean pollution: robot fish. These robot fish can swim around ocean habitats and measure pollution levels. The robot fish have tiny sensors that collect data on pollution in the ocean. Once in place, they will send the data to scientists back on land.

Robotic fish, such as this one, help scientists gather lots of information about ocean habitats.

KIDS CAN MAKE A DIFFERENCE

A group of students in Culebra, Puerto Rico, is pitching in to help protect the ocean. By joining the Ocean **Conservation** Youth Corps, these young people take part in important field research. This youth group, known as CORALations, works to help save the Caribbean coral reef habitat.

Students ages 10 to 18 take part in hands-on activities to help preserve ocean species. One of the group's main projects is helping to restore coral **reefs**. The group also has held all-night turtle watches to monitor sea turtle nests. The students learn about different species and the importance of protecting the oceans. Youth Corps members then share their knowledge with other students and with adults. They talk to their communities about what they have learned.

CORALations protects this coral reef to keep it bright and beautiful.

This photo shows fishermen working at a fish farm. Eating farmed fish will help protect ocean food chains.

CHOOSE YOUR FISH WISELY

Choosing the right seafood also can help protect ocean food chains. Some types of seafood are at risk from **overfishing**. Limit how much of this fish you eat. Instead, choose **sustainable** seafood. Sustainable seafood is raised or caught in a way that does not put the population at risk. Sustainable fishing operations take in smaller catches and avoid overfishing. Sustainable fish farms raise fish without destroying land or using up too many resources.

The Monterey Bay Aquarium website (see page 47) provides good information about which fish are safe to eat in different areas of the United States.

SPREAD THE WORD

Learn as much as you can about the amazing plants and animals that live in the water and take steps to protect them. Then share your knowledge with others. Together we can make a difference!

TOP 10 THINGS YOU CAN DO TO PROTECT OCEANS

There are lots of things you can do to protect ocean food chains and **habitats**. Here are 10 to start with:

1 Buy **organically** grown food, if possible. Support farms that do not use chemicals. These can **pollute** groundwater or rivers and make their way to the ocean.

2 Leave rare fish where they belong. Don't buy wild-caught saltwater fish for your aquarium.

3 Look but don't touch. Don't touch coral **reefs** or marine life. When visiting the beach, leave crabs in rock pools. Keep your distance from nesting birds.

4 Keep beaches and oceans clean and free of litter. Don't ever toss waste in the ocean or into other bodies of water.

5 Hold a bake sale or raffle. Raise money for **conservation** groups that protect oceans and ocean creatures, such as the World Wildlife Fund.

6 Choose **sustainable** seafood. Buy and eat only seafood that is farmed or caught in a way that preserves fish stocks for the future.

7 Never dump chemicals such as paints down the drain. They can damage ocean habitats.

8 Take part in beach clean-ups, if you live near a beach or plan to visit one.

9 Say no to plastic bags. Seabirds and sea turtles swallow them or get tangled in them and drown. Bring a reusable cloth bag to the store whenever you shop.

10 Get smart. Learn as much as you can about ocean food chains. Tell your friends and family everything that you have learned.

GLOSSARY

adapt when a species undergoes changes that help it survive

adaptation feature that helps a living thing survive

alien animal or plant that is brought by people to a new environment

anus part of the body that releases waste (poo)

bacteria simple, one-celled living things

bioluminescence living thing's ability to produce its own light

camouflage disguise that helps a creature hide

carnivore animal that eats only other animals

chlorophyll chemical that makes plants green and helps them trap sunlight energy

climate weather conditions in an area

climate change human-made changes in weather patterns

conservation protecting and saving the natural environment

consumer animal that cannot make its own food

crude oil oil that has not been processed into something usable

crustacean shrimplike animal with a hard skeleton covering the outside of its body

current movement of water in a river or ocean

decomposer living thing that breaks down dead plant and animal matter

diatom small type of phytoplankton

energy power needed to grow, move, and live

feces solid waste from an animal

frond a large leaf that divides into smaller sections

global warming worldwide increase in air and ocean temperature

habitat place where organisms of the same kind live

herbivore living things that eat only plants

holdfast growth when a plant clings to something

krill type of zooplankton that is a small crustacean

larvae young stage of insects and other animals that does not resemble an adult

native plant or animal that lives in the place it is adapted to

nutrient substance a living thing needs to live or grow

omnivore animal that eats both plants and animals

organic made in a natural way or containing only natural materials

organism living thing

overfishing when so many fish are caught from the same area that their numbers become very low or extinct

GLOSSARY

photosynthesis process plants use to turn sunlight into energy

phytoplankton tiny plants that live in the ocean; plant plankton

plankton small ocean organisms

pollute release harmful waste into the land, air, or water

pollution harmful waste

predator animal that eats another animal

prey animal that is eaten by another animal

primary consumer animal that feeds on plants, or producers; it is above the producers in the food chain

producer plant; first level of the food chain

reef system of corals, or tiny animals that leave behind shells over time

scavenger animal that feeds on dead matter

secondary consumer ocean predator; it feeds on primary consumers

species type of plant or animal

sustainable something that is done in a way that does not use up resources

tertiary consumer third-level consumer, or animal that feeds on animals that eat other animals

toxic poisonous

zooplankton tiny, floating ocean animals; animal plankton

FIND OUT MORE

BOOKS

Crossingham, John, and Bobbie Kalman. *Seashore Food Chains* (*Food Chain*). New York: Crabtree, 2005.

MacAulay, Kelley, and Bobbie Kalman. *Coral Reef Food Chains* (*Food Chain*). New York: Crabtree, 2005.

Tarbox, A. D. *An Ocean Food Chain* (*Nature's Bounty*). North Mankato, Minn.: Creative Education, 2009.

Wojahn, Rebecca Hogue, and Donald Wojahn. *A Coral Reef Food Chain: A Who-Eats-What Adventure in the Caribbean Sea* (*Follow That Food Chain*). Minneapolis: Lerner, 2010.

WEBSITES

www.education.noaa.gov/socean.html
This National Oceanic and Atmospheric Organization (NOAA) website features lots of fun activities for students.

http://magma.nationalgeographic.com/ngexplorer/0304/adventures/
Explore Australia's Great Barrier Reef on this National Geographic Kids website.

www.montereybayaquarium.org
Read about sustainable seafood on the Monterey Bay Aquarium website. Learn which fish and shellfish are safe to eat and which you should avoid.

FURTHER RESEARCH

Choose a topic from this book you'd like to research further. Do you live near an ocean you would like to know more about? Or is there a faraway ocean you think is exotic? Was there a creature in this book you find interesting? Is there something harming ocean food chains you'd like to know more about putting a stop to? Visit your local library to find out more information.

INDEX